Food Snobbery

An Intersectional Analysis of Fat, Feminism, Poverty, Disability & Health

Philippa Willitts

People are very passionate about food. This is understandable, because when it's good it can provide valuable nutrients to our body as well as cherished pleasure to our palates. But passion can become zeal and, before you know it, people are telling others how to eat. They are often well-meaning, when they evangelise about how easy it is to cut out gluten or become vegan, or how evil supermarkets or plastic packaging are, but they do not take into account the reality of many people's lives.

The line between food enthusiasts and food snobs can be a thin one, and when, "It's easier!", "It's cheaper!", etc. drown out your insistence that the intersecting oppressions of disability, poverty, racism and fat-phobia play a part, then that line has been crossed.

I was vegetarian for many years and I have to admit that I was obnoxious about it when I was a young teen. I would gleefully point out that anyone with meat on their plate was "eating a dead animal" and, although I was half-joking, I'm sure it made me a thoroughly unpleasant person to eat with. Thankfully, I grew out of that particularly objectionable habit long before adulthood, but many adults continue to judge others on what they eat as if it was a simple choice between good and bad with no other context.

In fact, there are so many nuances to the food that people have access to and choose to eat that it is impossible to simplify it. Even people with very strong views on which foods are 'good' and which are 'bad' cannot agree amongst themselves. Is veganism the only ethical choice, or are wheat and sugar that the worst things a person can put in their mouth? Is meat ok if it's organic? Should everything be eaten raw?

How do you best define "real" food?

- I can pronounce all of the ingredients on the label.
- Food that is minimally processed.
- Food I make at home.
- Food that doesn't come from a drive-thru..
- Food that doesn't contain refined grains or sweeteners.
- Other (please comment below).

Cast Your Vote

A food website attempts to define 'real' food[1]

Food snobbery is not limited to diets that might be considered by some to be "extreme". Trends for appreciating artisanal and exotic foods may please those who enjoy them, but using this "foodie" culture to shame people who buy cheap food does stigmatise those who do not limit their diet to corn-fed, cruelty-free parsnips.

Because along with food choices come judgements.

Whether a diet excludes a lot of foods or makes an effort to include others, people who cannot indulge in it, whether through an inability to afford ingredients, a lack of experience in cooking them or equipment to prepare them, a need to avoid certain foods or ingredients, or a simple dislike or lack of enjoyment, are vilified and criticised.

So, to start, what is food snobbery?

Adam Biagini wrote in Arts London News that, "The mark of a food snob is quite different from the mark of someone who loves food. [...] There's no denying that to the food lover, the farmers' market can offer an array of edible delights, but the food lover does the good thing and enjoys these things at face value, recognising how lucky he is to be eating so well.

"The food snob, on the other hand sees the farmers' market as a sign of his cultured, worldly aura, attempting to project a larger cultural context and sense of social status onto the £10 fromage du merde"[2].

---

[1] http://www.bestfoodfacts.org/food-for-thought/define_real_food

There isn't even a consistent way of doing it "correctly".

Michelle Allison, the Fat Nutritionist, writes that, "For some people, REAL FOOD means 'food I make entirely at home from scratch [for varying values of 'from scratch.']' For some, it means 'mainly plant-based foods with a smattering of dairy and animal protein.' For others, it means 'entirely raw foods that have not been cooked.' And for yet others, it might mean anything from 'a vegetarian diet' to 'mostly meat and certain vegetables and no grains' to 'a vegan diet composed entirely of homemade food' to 'I grow everything I eat on my own land, including grains which I mill into flour myself and then deep-fry unrepentantly.'

"There is a lot of wiggle-room in this term"[3].

Lately, there has been a lot of talk about "clean" food, as if all other food has been dropped on a grubby floor and put straight back onto the plate. And even when using the same terminology, there is no coherent meaning. The most arbitrary definition I have read is that real food has no more than six ingredients, but why six? What makes five ingredients real but seven fake? There are also declarations that meat, dairy, salt, sugar and white flour are all actually dangerous and poisonous[45], when they are demonstrably, well, *not poisonous*.

A proponent of the raw food diet, Esme Stevens, explains that, "Eating cooked food is eating dead food. This will make you feel heavy and tired"[6].

While Karen Knowler, "the raw food coach", explains that raw food

2   http://www.artslondonnews.com/2013/11/01/you-are-what-you-eat-middle-class-food-snobbery/

3 http://www.fatnutritionist.com/index.php/real-food/

4 http://www.waoy.org/32.html

5http://www.telegraph.co.uk/foodanddrink/healthyeating/9987825/Sweet-poison-why-sugar-is-ruining-our-health.html

6 http://www.thebestofrawfood.com/raw-food-diet.html

makes our bodies, "replac[e] our cells and bloodstream with cleaner, better nourished more 'alive' cells"[7], as if my poor, tortured, I-had-cooked-pasta-for-lunch cells are filthy and dying.

She goes on, "You will realise that you feel calmer, more in control, more harmonious in your thoughts and feelings, and you might even find yourself singing for no apparent reason (I kid you not!). This is simply a knock-on effect from the joy and equilibrium that your body is starting to experience through being fed the foods that suit it best".

So when I feel stressed, out of control or feel a lack of harmony, it's my own fault for boiling my veg. Right.

Others disguise judgement as pity, which is just as oppressive and unpleasant as blatant judgements, especially for disabled people experienced in the art of being pitied[8].

Food blogger Zoe Saint-Paul remarks, "There's a grocery store nearby that I occasionally go to for certain items where many local people do their food shopping. I can't count the number of times I've had tears in my eyes when I see what customers are buying. My husband says I shouldn't be so nosy... but when I see tired, depressed faces, obese bodies, people who look older than their age, and then I look at what's in their carts, I want to do something. Like grab those jumbo packs of soda, those cases of Little Debbies, and start running. I want to yell, "You're killing yourself!" and hand them some swiss chard. I've considered printing up flyers and putting them on cars in the parking lot"[9].

To counter the misinformation and the moral judgements, it seems wise to start with a straight-forward definition of "real food", so I will go with Sam Vance's suggestion that, "Real food is anything you eat and digest that offers calories and/or nutrition (carbs,

---

[7] http://therawfoodcoach.com/why-raw-benefits/

[8] http://www.copower.org/models-of-disability/178-tragedycharity-model-of-disability.html

[9] http://slowmama.com/fooddrink/whats-a-food-snob/

vitamins, proteins, fats)".[10]

From there, if you feel strongly that you don't want to eat any animal products, then become a vegan. If you feel more energetic when you avoid food with white flour, then cut it out. And if you love fresh vegetable juices every morning, then fill your boots. But don't impose those preferences on others.

As Michelle Allison explains, "The problem is that I've met very few people who make personal choices of the "real food" persuasion without ALSO pressuring those around them... without ALSO proclaiming that the foods most people rely on to survive are inherently inferior... without ALSO implying that the reason the rest of us are fat, or poor, or don't have shiny hair, or don't walk around perpetually bathed in magical sunbeams of happiness, is entirely because we eat the terrible, horrible, no-good, very bad food — the food that is not Real"[11].

So, when you're tempted to describe someone's lunch as, "garbage in a processed slice of plastic-wrapped cheese"[12], consider the Healthful Mama's apology to people she has previously judged for their food choices[13]. It highlights just how many of the limitations that can get in the way of eating "correctly" are regularly dismissed as a simple lack of will:

"'I can do it, so you can too,' they say, ignoring the fact that 'I' and 'you' are different people who face their own limitations and issues that may not neatly map over"[14].

---

[10] http://edibleintelligence.blogspot.co.uk/2010/03/real-food.html

[11] http://www.fatnutritionist.com/index.php/real-food/

[12] http://www.ahealthysliceoflife.com/2013/06/12/dont-be-a-food-snob/

[13] http://healthfulmama.com/2013/03/confessions-of-a-former-food-snob-i-owe-some-apologies/

[14] http://meloukhia.net/2013/10/foodies_get_over_your_personal_responsibility_hang up/

Disabled people often face serious barriers to eating well, for a multitude of reasons that will be explored here. Poverty, physical inaccessibility, social exclusion and other intersecting oppressions cannot be looked at individually; instead, a comprehensive approach must be taken.

Food and disability

Food and health are inherently connected, because what we consume can have a positive, neutral or negative impact on our bodies and minds. Disability – understood as the "restrictions caused by society when it does not give equivalent attention and accommodation to the needs of individuals with impairments"[15] – adds many more dimensions to the issue of what we eat, and how we eat it.

For some disabled people, eating ready-meals and pre-prepared food is the only way they can live independently. Others would like a more varied diet but, due to requiring assistance from shop assistants, find it, "easier to keep to a regular list (with the consequent sense of monotony) rather than entering into dialogue about new options"[16].

Disabled people who are institutionalised or hospitalised might have little, if any, control over their food intake at all.

Combined with limited funding, and the tendency of certain institutions to infantilise disabled people, this can mean they eat a disproportionate amount of food that is highly processed, or meals that are commonly associated with children (fish fingers, sausages and baked beans, for instance, although this will vary from culture to culture).

This paternalistic approach is incredibly disempowering, with disabled people being, "perceived and maintained as perpetual children"[17]. Criticising these people's diets as unhealthy, unnatural or "fake" is particularly offensive given the lack of choice many

[15] http://disability-studies.leeds.ac.uk/files/library/thomas-pam-Defining-Impairment-within-the-Social-Model-of-Disability.pdf

[16] http://www.food.gov.uk/multimedia/pdfs/disabilityandfood.pdf

[17] http://dsq-sds.org/article/view/19/19

residents of such places have.

Poverty is also a significant factor in the foods that disabled people eat.

Disability is expensive, and poverty leads to disability, so a vicious cycle is born that is impossibly challenging to break out of, especially because many disabled people are unable to work or are discriminated against in the job market. Even those in work face financial difficulty and food insecurity due to the costs associated with being disabled.

A report by the US Department of Agriculture (USDA) found that, "Even households that have incomes greater than three times the poverty level have a relatively high likelihood of being food insecure if they include an adult with a disability".[18]

Certain health conditions themselves can severely limit a person's food choices. Diabetes, Crohn's Disease, migraines, food allergies and Irritable Bowel Syndrome, for example, can all have an impact.

Medication, too, can have an effect on food choices. Certain anti-depressants (MAOIs) mean a person cannot eat cheese or drink red wine; grapefruit can cause toxicity when consumed with a long list of common medicines[19]; green leafy vegetables can have a dangerous effect when eaten while taking warfarin[20]; and bananas and salt substitutes can cause problems when ingested with certain heart medications[21].

This will impact, too, a disabled person's ability to socialise.

---

[18]   http://www.ers.usda.gov/amber-waves/2013-may/disability-is-an-important-risk-factor-for-food-insecurity.aspx#.UtzeKBBFDIU

[19]http://www.nhs.uk/news/2012/11November/Pages/Prescription-pills-and-grapefruit-a-deadly-mix.aspx

[20] http://www.eatright.org/Public/content.aspx?id=6442477646

[21]
http://www.fda.gov/downloads/Drugs/ResourcesForYou/Consumers/BuyingUsingMedicineSafely/EnsuringSafeUseofMedicine/GeneralUseofMedicine/UCM229033.pdf

For people using feeding tubes, this effect is particularly pronounced. Elaine Gerber explains how far-reaching the culture of eating out is, saying, "Given the cultural and biological importance of food, this includes nearly every social encounter: from the business lunch, to networking opportunities, to ritualized and religious events. People are financially and socially disadvantaged by an inability to 'break bread' together".[22]

---

[22] http://dsq-sds.org/article/view/19/19

Disability and access to food

A woman on Twitter recently accused me "subsidising capitalism" when I expressed dismay at having to go to a supermarket because my local vegetarian co-operative is inaccessible. I asked her what I should do instead and she said I should campaign for accessible local shops. And in the meantime, what? I don't eat?

It is this kind of unwillingness to look at the bigger picture that leads many people to feel that 'good', 'real' or 'clean' food campaigns are elitist and exclusive. Whether looking at food shops or places to eat out, it is a sad truth that many of the least physically-accessible locations are those that are independent and "ethical", while the multi-nationals we all love to hate are the ones with level access, wide open aisles, priority parking spaces and accessible toilets.

Non-disabled allies need to join disabled activists in proactively challenging the idea that a business can be considered to be ethical if it does not allow disabled customers to use it.

Good transport access to food shops and restaurants is also vital for disabled people to be able to get the food they need. Public transport must be accessible as well as available, and many people rely on expensive taxis if they struggle to hold or carry the goods they buy.

Shopping online isn't always a viable alternative: as well as requiring somebody to have internet access, a report by AbilityNet showed that the major British supermarkets fail to provide sufficiently accessible websites[23].

Once a disabled person has found a food shop that they can use, there are more barriers still. Many people with sensory impairments and learning disabilities find food labels impossible to navigate. It is difficult to identify the right products, and trying to decode the

---

[23] http://www.abilitynet.org.uk/news/little-christmas-cheer-for-disabled-people

nutritional information is another enormous obstacle. This makes attempts to "eat healthily", by reducing fat, salt or sugar, disproportionately difficult for many disabled people who cannot read or comprehend what the label says.

These same labels can cause problems at home. Reading and understanding cooking instructions, printed in a tiny font and crammed into a small space, poses problems not just for visually impaired people but also those whose first language is British Sign Language (BSL), whose grammatical structures and words differ from English. People with cognitive impairments, learning disabilities and mental health, memory and concentration problems can also be tripped up by overly-complicated cooking guidance, including technical language and abbreviations[24].

It is little wonder, then, that many disabled people choose food that is simple and familiar. Elaine Gerber explains that, "foods that are easy to prepare or acquire are also often the same ones that deserve criticism for their nutritional shortcomings"[25].

Buying some ready-prepared food puts me automatically in the 'not-real food' bracket for many, because it is:

a)   in a packet, and
b)   processed.

But even though I prefer home-cooked food, this is sometimes a necessity. As a single person, buying ready-prepared fruit salads gives me a variety of fruits that I would not be able to buy individually without waste, and as a disabled person I can't always chop and prepare and stir and cook. Impaired manual dexterity, concentration, vision or cognitive capacity can all make food preparation potentially dangerous, and some people who self-harm are simply not able to handle the triggers associated with dealing with sharp knives and heat sources safely.

There is equipment available that can help disabled people to prepare

24 http://www.food.gov.uk/multimedia/pdfs/disabilityandfood.pdf

25 http://dsq-sds.org/article/view/19/19

food independently, but it is often extremely expensive. A one-handed chopping board cost me £75, when I could have paid £1 for a regular one, and to equip a kitchen with an array of special knives, plates, pans, cups etc. would be prohibitively expensive for the vast majority of people. The alternative? A £3 ready meal and a microwave. Or a takeaway, a sandwich, or a packet of crisps. None of which pass muster with food snobs.

Disability intersects with poverty, racism and fat-phobia

According to the Church Action on Poverty and Oxfam, "around 13 million people are in poverty in the UK. […] At least four million of them suffer from food poverty", meaning, "an individual or household isn't able to obtain healthy, nutritious food – they have to eat what they can afford, not what they choose to"[26].

As we have seen, disability and poverty are inextricably linked.

The USDA explains why disability can have such a significant impact on a person's finances: "Disabilities often lead to reductions in earnings for the person with a disability and for other household members who may need to care for the individual with a disability. Monetary expenses related to health care, adaptive equipment, such as wheelchairs or special telephones, and other expenses associated with disability may result in an increased likelihood of food insecurity. […] A study by Mathematica Policy Research found that a person with a persistent work-limiting disability would require more than two and half times the income of an able-bodied person to have the same likelihood of food insecurity. Individuals with disabilities may also have difficulty shopping for food, preparing healthy meals, and managing food resources."[27]

The need for food banks in recent years has increased massively in the UK, as a direct result of the government's brutal cuts to benefits and rising food prices.

The Disability Benefits Consortium found that 15% of disabled

[26]http://www.church-poverty.org.uk/walkingthebreadline/info/report/walkingthebreadlinefile

[27]   http://www.ers.usda.gov/amber-waves/2013-may/disability-is-an-important-risk-factor-for-food-insecurity.aspx#.UtzeKBBFDIU

people who have had their Housing Benefit cut and an increase in their contribution to Council Tax "have had to rely on food banks as a result"[28]. This effectively reduces the choices people are able to make about their food to zero.

Whether it is a lack of healthcare, bad living conditions, avoiding the expense of heating a home, poor access to food or the stress of never having enough money, it is undeniable that poverty increases a person's chances of becoming disabled.

Church Action on Poverty has found that, "The rising cost of living combined with austerity cuts is forcing poor families to choose whether to pay their bills or put food on the table; research has found that parents are regularly going without food in order to feed their children.

And a recent survey found that one in five mothers regularly go without meals so that their children can eat, 16% are being treated for stress-related illnesses (due to financial worries), and one third are borrowing money from friends and family to stay afloat"[29].

The Food Trust has identified that, "many low-income communities, communities of color, and sparsely populated rural areas do not have sufficient opportunities to buy healthy, affordable food. The consequences are clear: decreased access to healthy food means people in low-income communities suffer more from diet-related diseases like obesity and diabetes than those in higher-income neighborhoods"[30].

It is clear that financial difficulties can put an extreme strain on a person's health and wellbeing, but it is also the case that being disabled can also lead to financial difficulties, thanks to poor employment opportunities or an inability to work at all, limited

---

[28]   http://disabilitybenefitsconsortium.wordpress.com/2013/12/17/food-banks-become-lifeline-for-disabled-people-as-benefit-changes-hit/

[29]http://www.church-poverty.org.uk/walkingthebreadline/info/report/walkingthebreadlinefile

[30] http://thefoodtrust.org/uploads/media_items/grocerygap.original.pdf

access to education, and higher expenditure on adapted or specially-designed items which invariably cost a lot more. Foods to cater for special dietary needs can be obscenely expensive when compared to their non-specialist counterparts, and the ongoing need to spend more on heating, clothing, taxis, and personal care account for a considerable amount of money overall.

All of this can create an inescapable situation where each thing exacerbates the next, leading to an unbearable downward spiral.

One client at an Advice Centre in Manchester reported, "My depression has worsened considerably, and the reduced amount I have to spend on food is affecting my diabetes and blood pressure. I also have more frequent panic attacks when thinking about our finances"[31].

When a passionate vegan says that people in poverty should all be vegans, because buying fresh vegetables and cooking from scratch is so much cheaper, it might initially make sense. Grabbing a handful of potatoes, carrots and onions in a local market could be the basis of several hearty meals for less than the price of a single takeaway or shop-bought sandwich.

But, as ever, things are not that simple.

That scenario assumes that:

- a person has a market nearby
- there is accessible parking at, or accessible public transport to, the market
- the market itself is physically accessible
- a person is safe to peel, chop and cook food
- a person understands how to peel, chop and cook food
- a person has pans, a stove and a wooden spoon
- a person has enough credit left in their electricity meter to cook a meal.

---

[31]http://www.church-poverty.org.uk/walkingthebreadline/info/report/walkingthebreadlinefile

In one of the most depressing news stories of 2013, clients of British food banks were reported to be, "giving back food items that need cooking because they can't afford to turn on the electricity"[32].

There is also the counter-intuitive but ruthless fact that things cost more when you are poor, whether that is metered household fuel, less ability to take advantage of "3 for the price of 2" special offers, and more expensive bank and credit services.

On top of this, food prices, "have risen by 30.5% in the last five years; this is double the rate of inflation, and two and a half times the rate of increases in the National Minimum Wage.

"People are spending more on food but eating less: expenditure on food and non-alcoholic beverages has increased by almost 20% in the last five years, but the volume of food being consumed has fallen by 7%. It is predicted that the average food bill will increase by £257 over the next five years, further increasing the number of people affected by food poverty"[33].

And, just as poverty intersects with disability, these oppressions intersect with others, too.

Low-income communities of color in the US are particularly vulnerable to a lack of decent food provision in local shops. For instance, "in Baltimore, 46 percent of lower-income neighborhoods have limited access to healthy food (based on a healthy food availability survey) compared to 13 percent of higher-income neighborhoods"[34].

These combined oppressions also intersect with fat-phobia. The 'rules' of food snobbery are often imposed on fat people in particular,

[32]   http://www.bloomberg.com/news/2013-10-15/u-k-food-bank-users-return-what-needs-cooking-as-demand-triples.html?utm_content=buffer5afd0&utm_source=buffer&utm_medium=twitter&utm_campaign=Buffer

[33]http://www.church-poverty.org.uk/walkingthebreadline/info/report/walkingthebreadlinefile

[34] http://thefoodtrust.org/uploads/media_items/grocerygap.original.pdf

based on the array of assumptions and judgements that are made about us.

And needing healthcare when fat can be very costly.

Lesley Kinzel explains that, "not all medical equipment is made to accommodate larger bodies -- even a necessary diagnostic MRI can be become a challenge to get if your body is too heavy for the machine at the facility your health insurance will cover.

[...]

"Costs may also be higher because fat people, especially fat women, are less likely to have preventative care -- or even regular cancer screenings for gynecological and colon cancers -- that may catch life-threatening issues before they become, well, life-threatening. The tangible result of this reluctance is that by the time many fat women do get treatment, what might have been a simple thing six months ago is now a much more serious matter to correct"[35].

She concludes, "All that the current atmosphere around fatness does is reinforce the social issues that keep fat people poor and sick"[36].

---

[35] http://www.xojane.com/issues/obesity-economics

[36] http://www.xojane.com/issues/obesity-economics

Bad advice

Just as the pressure from food snobs, real foodists and 'clean' food advocates can be oppressive in its patronising superiority, the benefits of these diets are not even clear cut.

Michelle Allison writes, "The reality is, even foods we tend to recognize as universally wholesome and healthy are not actually appropriate for everyone. Bodies differ and circumstances also differ. For example, our universally beloved super food, dark leafy greens, are considered a food to avoid (along with a bunch of other "healthy" foods like whole grains, legumes, and many fruits and vegetables) for people with kidney disease who require a low potassium diet.

"Eating MORE sodium instead of less sodium can actually be a critical thing for people who experience hypotension — when I was working in the hospital, we actually had to stop purchasing a popular brand of bouillon for this purpose when they lowered the sodium in their product in an attempt to provide a healthier option to consumers. Well, it wasn't healthier for our patients on tube feeds, some of whom required a sodium boost between feedings — in fact it was quite dangerous"[37].

Blogger Christopher Wanjek has explained how at least some of the raw vegan diet is based on bad science[38]. He proposes that the "facts" used to promote the practice are either partially true, true but irrelevant or not credible or accurate at all, and that these kinds of diets can be damaging to the health[39]. Dr Mehmet Oz has clarified that frozen and canned foods can be more nutritious than their fresh counterparts[40], and even the benefits of eating organic are far from

---

[37] http://www.fatnutritionist.com/index.php/real-food/

[38] http://www.livescience.com/26278-risks-raw-vegan-diet.html

[39] http://www.livescience.com/26278-risks-raw-vegan-diet.html

clear-cut[41].

Michael Ruhlman reports that "a study that found that men with heart disease who REDUCED their intake of meat and saturated fats and INCREASED the polyunsaturated fats in their diet were MORE likely to die of a heart attack than the control group who maintained their customary diet. It noted the existence of a 'small but unsettling body of data suggesting that consuming polyunsaturated oils … may … increase your risk of heart disease'"[42], [43].

None of this is to say that you should abandon all hope of ever eating a genuinely healthy food again, just that, as with everything, there are nuances and there are things that we do not yet fully understand.

[40] http://www.healthcentral.com/diet-exercise/c/727598/157522/highlights/

[41] http://www.spiked-online.com/newsite/article/7222#.Utwu8hBFDIU

[42]http://ruhlman.com/2013/03/cook-your-own-food-eat-what-you-want-think-for-yourself/

[43]http://well.blogs.nytimes.com/2013/03/07/eat-your-heart-out/?_php=true&_type=blogs&_r=0

The problem exacerbates itself

When local shops aren't accessible, when fresh food isn't readily available and when it is expensive and poor quality, we are more likely to shop in supermarkets and chain stores.

It is well known that this, then, has a detrimental effect on small, independent, local businesses, who go out of business[44], creating 'food deserts' where poorer people only have access to food that is up to 69% more expensive[45] than the food available *in the same supermarket chain* in wealthier areas.

Further, independent shops employ five times as many people per unit of turnover than supermarkets do[46], so along with increased prices and lower quality food comes higher unemployment too, to intensify the problem even more.

Nobody but the massive corporations are gaining from the exclusivity of local indie stores, and yet those who are unable to use them are still held responsible for their inaccessibility.

---

[44]http://www.theguardian.com/commentisfree/2009/aug/10/tesco-planning-superstore-independent-shops

[45]http://www.church-poverty.org.uk/walkingthebreadline/info/report/walkingthebreadlinefile

[46]http://www.theguardian.com/commentisfree/2009/aug/10/tesco-planning-superstore-independent-shops

Conclusion

It is evident that the problem with "unhealthy" food is inherently structural within a discriminatory society. It is not a coincidence that so many more poor people, disabled people, and people of colour eat less balanced diets with more packaged food and less fresh produce, and it is not that these people are all careless and feckless and don't care what they put in their bodies.

This is a wider issue of structural inequality that cannot be addressed on an individual level. It is not just a matter of "personal responsibility".

Food snobbery, whether it manifests in lecturing, chiding, self-importance or dismissive comments, ignores the entirety of those circumstances to focus on one single thing: *you should not be eating that*.

There is no context and no nuance, so it makes no difference that the ardent raw fooder has enough garden space to grow her own vegetables, or that the guy opposing dairy consumption has access to an amazing little shop selling dairy alternatives.

These people apply principles to their food intake that, for a combination of reasons, they are able to fulfil. Their circumstances allow it. This is not to say that these diets don't sometimes involve an awful lot of willpower and determination – many of them do – but it is misguided to believe that that is all there is to it.

We need to look seriously at how messages from food evangelists, piled on top of all the other crap we are told about what we eat on an ongoing basis, are affecting the what we consume and how we judge other people.

Brendan O'Neill wrote in the Guardian, "Today's foodie fundamentalism – from TV shows that poke about in people's faeces to government advice on how much fruit and veg we should eat – is a deeply moralistic campaign dressed up as health advice. Behind the scientific gloss of offering people tips on nutritional content, there lurks a snobbish disdain for people's behaviour and values" [47].

And it's not like this kind of bullying is effective: have you known anyone make long-term changes to their eating habits based on being shamed or humiliated about their food choices?

Michelle Allison, in a blog post about "real food", wrote, "If food is keeping someone, somewhere alive, then it is real enough"[48], and understanding this, along with the truly intersectional nature of oppression, unfairness and discrimination in society, is the only way to even begin to address the real structures that enable such inequality and disparity to thrive.

[47] http://www.theguardian.com/commentisfree/2008/aug/27/oliver.foodanddrink

[48] http://www.fatnutritionist.com/index.php/real-food/

Bibliography

- Allison, Michelle. "**Real Food.**" THE FAT NUTRITIONIST, 11/11/2013.
- "**Avoid Food-Drug Interactions**." FOOD AND DRUG ADMINISTRATION.
- Bazian. "**Prescription drugs and grapefruit a 'deadly mix'.**" NHS CHOICES, 27/11/2012.
- Begun, Rachel. "**5 Common Food-Drug Interactions.**" ACADEMY OF NUTRITION AND DIETETICS, June 2013.
- Biagini, Adam. "**You are what you eat — middle class food snobbery.**" Arts London News, 1/11/13.
- Coleman-Jensen, Alisha and Nord, Mark. "**Disability Is an Important Risk Factor for Food Insecurity.**" USDA ECONOMIC RESEARCH SERVICE, 6/5/2013.
- Dixon, Brittany. "**Nobody Likes a Food Snob.**" A HEALTHY SLICE OF LIFE, 12/6/2013.
- Dorian, Martin. "**Time Magazine Highlights Dr. Oz's 'Anti-Food-Snob-Diet.'**" HEALTH CENTRAL, 27/11/2012.
- "**Food banks become lifeline for disabled people as benefits changes hit.**" DISABILITY BENEFITS CONSORTIUM, 17/12/2013.
- "Food for Thought Poll: How do you define 'real food'?" Food for Thought, 16/5/2012.
- Gerber, Elaine. "**Food Studies and Disability Studies: Introducing a Happy Marriage.**" DISABILITY STUDIES

QUARTERLY, Summer 2007, Volume 27, Number 3.

- Healthful Mama. "**Confessions of a Former Food Snob: I Owe Some Apologies.**" HEALTHFUL MAMA, 26/3/2013.
- Kinzel, Lesley. "**Maybe Fat People Are Poor And Sick Because Our Culture Treats Them Like Garbage.**" XOJANE, 17/1/2014.
- Knowler, Karen. "**Why Go Raw?**" THE RAW FOOD COACH.
- Lambert, Victoria. "**Sweet poison: why sugar is ruining our health.**" THE TELEGRAPH, 9/1/2014.
- Lyons, Rob. "**Organic food and unhealthy snobbery.**" Spiked Online, 3/8/2009.
- Malkmus, George. "**The Five White Poisons**."
- MICHIGAN DISABILITY RIGHTS COALITION. "**Tragedy/Charity Model of Disability.**"
- Monbiot, George. "**My town is menaced by a superstore. So why are we not free to fight it off?**" THE GUARDIAN, 10/8/2009.
- Niall, Cooper and Dumpleton, Sarah. "**Walking the Breadline.**" CHURCH ACTION ON POVERTY/OXFAM, May 2013.
- O'Neill, Brendan. "**Roasting the masses.**" THE GUARDIAN, 27/8/2008.
- Penny, Thomas. "**U.K. Food-Bank Users Return What Needs Cooking as Bills Rise.**" BLOOMBERG, 16/10/2013.
- Reynolds, Gretchen. "**Eat Your Heart Out.**" NEW YORK TIMES, 7/3/2013.
- Ruhlman, Michael. "**Cook Your Own Food. Eat Your Heart Out.**" MICHAEL RUHLMAN, 14/3/2013.
- Saint-Paul, Zoe. "**What's a food snob?**" SLOW MAMA, 2/5/2011.

- smith, s.e. "**Foodies, Get Over Your Personal Responsibility Hangup.**" this ain't livin', 15/10/2013."
- "**Social Research Around Disability and Food.**" CREATIVE RESEARCH, June 2007.
- Stevens, Esme. "**Raw Food Diet — FAQ.**" THE BEST OF RAW FOOD.
- Thomas, Pam, et al. "**Defining Impairment Within the Social Model of Disability.**" COALITION MAGAZINE, July 1997.
- Treuhaft, Sarah and Karpyn, Allison. "**The Grocery Gap.**" THE FOOD TRUST.
- Vance, Sam. "**Real Food.**" EDIBLE INTELLIGENCE, 2/3/2010.
- Walker, Mark. "**eNation: Supermarkets fail disabled people this Christmas**." ABILITYNET, 13/12/2013.
- Wanjek, Christopher. "**Reality Check: 5 Risks of Raw Vegan Diet.**" LIVESCIENCE, 15/1/2013.

Philippa Willitts is a feminist writer who is also the author of **Devoted: A Feminist Analysis of Disability Fetishism.**

This extended article appeared, in an earlier form, on www.disabilityintersections.com